Arduino Robot HowTo

Ricky KWAK

Table of Contents

Step 1. Arduino Development Environment

The goal of this book is to build a very basic autonomous robot using Arduino and sensor. It uses an Arduino Uno, two motors, an ultrasonic sensor, and a servo motor. The ultrasonic sensor measures distance and changes direction to move when it detects an object.

What is Arduino?

Arduino is an open-source, single-board microcontroller complete with a board and associated development tools and environment. It was invented in 2005 at the Interaction Design Institutelvera (IDII) in Italy to allow students unfamiliar with hardware to easily control their designs. (Wikipedia)

The Arduino can be used to control sensors, motors, or LEDs, allowing you to create interactive products with multiple connected sensors or motors. It can be developed in C language and provides an IDE. You need to know the basics of the C language to develop with Arduino. The binary code converted to machine language code is downloaded from the computer to the Arduino via serial communication. Nowadays, PCs do not have serial and use USB to Serial, which means that they are connected to each other using a USB cable, but the internal communication uses serial communication. The classification of Arduino is based on the MCU (Micro Controller Unit) used in the product, and the UNO is the most common for beginners.

Due to its popularity, Arduino is often used by companies for early development prototypes, and since the schematics of Arduino boards are open under the Creative Common License, anyone can build and modify them. Therefore, many companies use Arduino boards to test their products and modify the open schematics when they actually produce them.

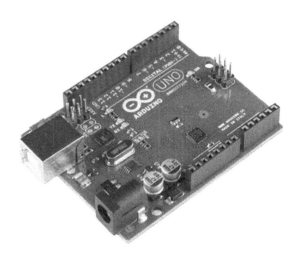

The official Arduino website is

https://www.arduino.cc/

You can sign up using your Google account to develop on the web, or you can download the application and develop on Chrome, but for this tutorial, we're going to set up our own development environment on a Windows PC. To develop code on the web, you need to sign up for the Arduino site. Once you're logged in, click the icon next to your account in the top right corner and select web Editor.

After selecting the web editor and following some instructions, you should see a web editor that looks like this. This is where you can develop your own code. You can also get upgraded features for a monthly fee.

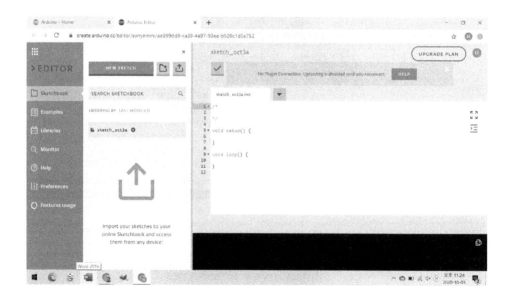

IDE installation and default settings

From the Arduino home page, go to Software → Downloads and you'll find a link to download the Arduino IDE. Since I'm using Windows, I selected "Windows app Requires Win 8.1 or 10". As the page progresses, you'll see the option to "Just Download" or "Contribute & Download" which allows you to download with a donation. If you choose "Just Download" you will be directed to the Microsoft Store, click on the free install and the IDE will install automatically.

Once you select the installed Arduino IDE, you will see the following IDE window.

Using an Arduino gives you the opportunity to use boards other than the UNO board, depending on your application. For example, you might want to use a Wi-Fi enabled board with your Arduino board. In each case, you will need to select the appropriate board. In the Arduino IDE, you can see the board information by selecting the Tools menu at the top, as shown in the following image. The next most important thing is the port information. These are the ports you use to connect your Arduino to your PC and download software.

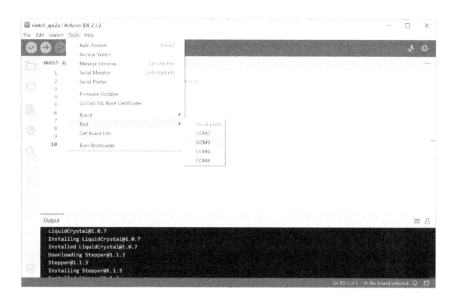

Since we will be using an Arduino UNO board, there is no additional setup required. Developing with Arduino doesn't take much effort once you have the IDE installed. The coding is simple as well as the structure of the code.

Arduino makes it very easy to create a working project if you know the C language. The C language is hard to explain in a page or two, but the Arduino code is not complicated, so you can type while reading the book, so it will make sense as you build the code. If you have any questions, you can Google it and learn it one by one. Since we are using only the most basic code of the C language, watching an hour or two of YouTube videos will also be very helpful.

Step 2. Create a robot

This chapter, we'll actually start coding and implementing the behavior we want. You will need to purchase the parts needed to build your robot using sites like Amazon.

What kind of robot should we build?

You will build a robot that uses motor control to move two wheels and ultrasonic sensors to avoid obstacles in front of it. In addition to the Arduino Uno board, you will need the following materials

- 4 motors and 4 wheels each
- Servo motor (SG90)
- Ultrasonic sensor (HC-SR04)
- Motor Drive Controller (L298N)
- One each of 1k, 2k resistors and 470uF 25V capacitor
- Two 18650 batteries and battery holder
- PCB support bolts
- Dupont cable
- Acrylic (material for the robot's body)

Motors and wheels   Servo motors   Ultrasonic sensors

Motor Driver   Battery Holder   Battery

PCB Support   Dupont Cable

Make the Motor Run

The motor runs on 3V, and if you change the direction of the power, reversing the + and - connections will change the direction of rotation. We will be using something called a motor drive. The Arduino also has a 5V or 3.3V output pin, but we can't use it because of the low output of the Arduino board. So we'll use a motor drive called the L298N, and we'll connect a separate power source to the motor drive and get a digital signal from the Arduino to run the motor.

 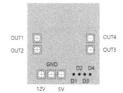

In the previous figure, the motor drive 298N has two connection terminals on the left and right side, which are connected to the motor respectively. This means that two motors can be connected to one 298N. At the bottom, you can see three connections and four digital input pins. The first of the three connections is the 12V input. You can connect up to 24V, and we're going to use 7V as our input. And the 7V used as the input of the 298N will be connected to the 5V input of the Arduino, which we can do by connecting the Arduino pin to Vin. This serves the same purpose as connecting to the Arduino power source. The four pins on the bottom right can accept digital inputs, with D1 and D2 controlling the motors on the left and D3 and D4 controlling the motors on the right. The two digital input pins work as a pair, with HIGH, LOW making the motor rotate in the forward direction, LOW, HIGH making it reverse, and HIGH, HIGH making it stop.

The final pin and input connections for the motor, Arduino, and motor drive are shown in the previous figure. The red and black cables at the bottom will be connected to the battery with + and - respectively. We're going to do our first bit of coding to make the motor run. I'll provide the source for you, but I recommend typing it out to get a feel for it. To make sure the pins are connected correctly, I wrote the following code.

I declared variables to assign the pins. I connected pins D1 through D4 on the board to digital pins 2 through 5 on the Arduino, respectively. I declared the digital pins and assigned each pin number.

Then the code will be as below.

```
AutoRobot | Arduino IDE 2.3.2                                    —   □   ×
File  Edit  Sketch  Tools  Help

  ⊘  →  ⊗      Select Board          ▼                          ∧  ⊙

  AutoRobot.ino                                                      ...

   17   /*|
   18    * Init function, start arduino then only one run automatically
   19    */
   20   void setup() {
   21     // wheel pin mode define
   22     pinMod(LeftWheel_D1, OUTPUT);
   23     pinMod(LeftWheel_D2, OUTPUT);
   24     pinMod(RightWheel_D3, OUTPUT);
   25     pinMod(RightWheel_D4, OUTPUT);
   26
   27     // all of wheel set to stop status
   28     digitalWrite(LeftWheel_D1, HIGH);
   29     digitalWrite(LeftWheel_D2, HIGH);
   30     digitalWrite(RightWheel_D3, HIGH);
   31     digitalWrite(RightWheel_D4, HIGH);
   32
   33     // sleep 1 second
   34     delay(1000)
   35   }
   36
   37   void loop(){
   38     digitalWrite(LeftWheel_D1, HIGH);
   39     digitalWrite(LeftWheel_D2, LOW);
   40     digitalWrite(RightWheel_D3, HIGH);
   41     digitalWrite(RightWheel_D4, LOW);
   42   }
                                    Ln 17, Col 3   ✕ No board selected  ᐃ
```

Next up are the setup and loop functions. The setup is a function that is executed only once when the Arduino starts up and contains all the initialization code. The loop function is a function that is repeated indefinitely while the Arduino is powered up. In the previous code, the setup function uses a function called pinMode to declare that all four pins are used for output. We set them to OUTPUT because we will be controlling the motor by outputting HIGH and LOW respectively. The input pins can be defined as INPUT. Next, we wrote HIGH to each pin using the digitalWrite function. When all of the HIGHs are output, the motor will stop.

Finally, the delay function is a pause function, and the unit of 1000 passed in as an argument is mile sec, which means to pause for 1 second. As described earlier, setup is automatically executed only once and then the loop is repeated infinitely. Inside the loop, we output HIGH to D1 and LOW to D2 to rotate the left motor in the forward direction and the right wheel in the forward direction in the same way. Once you've finished entering the code, connect the Arduino to your computer with a USB cable. After connecting the Arduino, go to Tools → Ports in the IDE and you should see additional ports besides the Com port and select the one with the Arduino UNO in parentheses. Once the Arduino is connected, select Upload from the sketch and the code will be compiled and uploaded to the Arduino. Once the upload is complete, you can disconnect the USB cable and plug it in.

If you get an error when compiling, find the cause and debug it.

Create a function

In the previous example, we put four lines of code in a loop to move the robot forward, but the robot will need to move backwards, turn left, turn right, and stop in addition to moving forward. For each of these, we need to add four lines of code. And I need to put HIGH or LOW in the digitalWrite function, which is hard to understand when I look at the code later. It's not easy to understand the code unless you memorize that D1 and D2 need HIGH to stop and HIGH and LOW to go forward. So we want to create functions for forward, backward, stop, left, and right, respectively, and call those functions.

```
AutoRobot | Arduino IDE 2.3.2                                    —    □    ×
File  Edit  Sketch  Tools  Help

  ⊘  →  ⊳      Select Board              ▼                          ᴧ  ·ϙ·

     AutoRobot.ino                                                       ...
        3    | *                     code by ricky.kwak
        4    | *                     2024.04.02
        5    | * * * * * * * * * * * * * * * * * * * * * * * * * * * * * */
        6
        7    | /*
        8    | * For two wheel digital input / ouput D1 to D4
        9    | * D1, D2 left wheel, D3, D4 right wheel
       10    | */
       11
       12    int LeftWheel_D1    =    2;
       13    int LeftWheel_D2    =    3;
       14    int RightWheel_D3   =    4;
       15    int rightWheel_D4   =    5;
       16
       17    /|
       18    | * each function for robot movement
       19    | */
       20    void Robot_Stop();
       21    void Robot_Go();
       22    void Robot_RightTurn();
       23    void Robot_LeftTurn();
       24    void Robot_Back();
       25
                                        Ln 17, Col 3   × No board selected  ⏸
```

After declaring the digital port number, we declare five functions. This declares the existence of these functions, and then we need to implement the behavior of each function. Here's what each one looks like.

```
/*
 * Stop Robot
 */
void Robot_Stop(){
  Serial.println("Stop Robot");
  digitalWrite(LeftWheel_D1, HIGH);
  digitalWrite(LeftWheel_D2, HIGH);
  digitalWrite(RightWheel_D3, HIGH);
  digitalWrite(RightWheel_D4, HIGH);
}

/*
 * Move to forward
 */
void Robot_Go(){
  Serial.println("Robot Forward");
  digitalWrite(LeftWheel_D1, HIGH);
  digitalWrite(LeftWheel_D2, LOW);
  digitalWrite(RightWheel_D3, HIGH);
  digitalWrite(RightWheel_D4, LOW);
}

/*
 * Right Turn
 */
void Robot_RightTurn(){
  Serial.println("Robot Right Turn");
  digitalWrite(LeftWheel_D1, HIGH);
  digitalWrite(LeftWheel_D2, HIGH);
  digitalWrite(RightWheel_D3, HIGH);
  digitalWrite(RightWheel_D4, LOW);
}

/*
 * Left Turn
 */
void Robot_LeftTurn(){
  Serial.println("Robot Left Turn");
  digitalWrite(LeftWheel_D1, HIGH);
  digitalWrite(LeftWheel_D2, LOW);
  digitalWrite(RightWheel_D3, HIGH);
  digitalWrite(RightWheel_D4, HIGH);
}
```

```
/*
 * Left Turn
 */
void Robot_LeftTurn(){
  Serial.println("Robot Left Turn");
  digitalWrite(LeftWheel_D1, HIGH);
  digitalWrite(LeftWheel_D2, LOW);
  digitalWrite(RightWheel_D3, HIGH);
  digitalWrite(RightWheel_D4, HIGH);
}

/*
 * Robot Move Back
 */
void Robot_Back(){
  Serial.println("Robot Move Back");
  digitalWrite(LeftWheel_D1, LOW);
  digitalWrite(LeftWheel_D2, HIGH);
  digitalWrite(RightWheel_D3, LOW);
  digitalWrite(RightWheel_D4, HIGH);
}
```

Here we see a function called Serial_println that we didn't see before. This is for debugging purposes so that we can use the Arduino's serial monitor to verify that each function call is being made. In order to use this serial output function, we need to initialize the serial, which is done in the setup function as follows, and we need to align the board at the bottom of the serial monitor to see the message.

```
29    void setup() {
30        // UART initialize for debugging
31        Serial.begin(115200);
32        Serial.println("")
33
34
35        // wheel pin mode define
36        pinMod(LeftWheel_D1, OUTPUT);
37        pinMod(LeftWheel_D2, OUTPUT);
38        pinMod(RightWheel_D3, OUTPUT);
39        pinMod(RightWheel_D4, OUTPUT);
40
41        // all of wheel set to stop status
42        digitalWrite(LeftWheel_D1, HIGH);
43        digitalWrite(LeftWheel_D2, HIGH);
44        digitalWrite(RightWheel_D3, HIGH);
45        digitalWrite(RightWheel_D4, HIGH);
46
47        // sleep 1 second
48        delay(1000)
49    }
50
51    void loop(){
```

And since we've created functions for each robot movement, we can change the setup and loop functions as follows

```
37        pinMod(LeftWheel_D2, OUTPUT);
38        pinMod(RightWheel_D3, OUTPUT);
39        pinMod(RightWheel_D4, OUTPUT);
40
41        // All the wheel change to stop status
42        Robot_Stop()
43
44        // sleep 1 second
45        delay(1000)
46    }
47
48    void loop(){
49        Robot_Go();
50        delay(1000);
51        Robot_RightTrun();
52        delay(1000);
53        Robot_LeftTurn();
54        delay(1000);
55        Robot_back();
56        delay(1000);
57        Robot_Stop();
58        delay(1000);
59    }
```

First, in the setup function, the four lines of code that initialized the robot to stop were simplified to one line. Also, the loop function was changed to monitor the behavior of the motors by calling the following actions: forward and pause for 1 second, right turn and pause for 1 second, left turn and pause for 1 second, backward and pause for 1 second, and stop the robot and pause for 1 second. Connect the Arduino to the PC, open the serial monitor to set the bottom port and board, and select upload in the IDE to send the binary to the Arduino. With the USB cable plugged in, power it up and you should see a message on the serial monitor. If you don't plug it in, the motors won't run, but you'll see messages on the serial monitor because there's not enough power going through the PC's USB port to the Arduino.

Servo motors

A servo motor is a motor that is used to move a specific angle based on a command from the CPU. There are three wires, usually red for power, black or brown for GND, and yellow or orange for data.

The servo motor is oriented 90 degrees to the front, so you can give it a number from 0 to 179 degrees and it will rotate for each degree. The reason we are using a servo motor is to attach an ultrasonic sensor to the axis of rotation. We want to have the ultrasonic sensor measure the distance at each angle of rotation and determine whether to move forward or backward based on the measured distance. The data line from the servo motor is connected to pin 6 of the Arduino. Here is a picture of the connection

To use a servo motor, we need to include Servo.h, which has the servo motor control functions. You can see that I added the relevant header file at

the top of the following source code. The data pin of the servo motor is assigned to number 6, and a variable servo of the servo motor type is declared. We control the servo motor through this object, and since the angle of the servo motor is based on 90 degrees to the front at startup, we declared a variable and assigned it 90.

```
AutoRobot | Arduino IDE 2.3.2                                    —    □    ×
File  Edit  Sketch  Tools  Help

  ✓  →  ▶    Select Board              ▼                              ⋀  ⊙

     AutoRobot.ino                                                          ...

      1   /* * * * * * * * * * * * * * * * * * * * * * * * * * * * * * * * * * * * * * *
      2    *              AutoRobot
      3    *                      code by ricky.kwak
      4    *                      2024.04.02
      5    * * * * * * * * * * * * * * * * * * * * * * * * * * * * * * * * * * * * * * */
      6   #include <Servo.h>
      7
      8   /*
      9    * For two wheel digital input / ouput D1 to D4
     10    * D1, D2 left wheel, D3, D4 right wheel
     11    */
     12
     13   int LeftWheel_D1   =   2;
     14   int LeftWheel_D2   =   3;
     15   int RightWheel_D3  =   4;
     16   int rightWheel_D4  =   5;
     17
     18   // Servo motor pin number
     19   int ServoPin = 6;
     20   Servo servo;
     21   int ServoAngle = 90;
     22
     23   /*|

                                          Ln 23, Col 3   × No board selected  ⌂
```

The next thing we need to do is initialize the servo motor in the setup function, using the servo object's attach function to tell the Arduino which pin the servo motor's data line is assigned to. In the code above, we see %, which is the remainder operator. When we do 5%3, we get the remainder of 5 divided by 3, which means the answer is 2. The loop then increments the angle every 45 degrees, and if the angle is less than 180, it rotates to that angle. To rotate, you can write the angle value to the servo object's write function. If it's less than 180, we divide the angle by 180 and subtract the remainder of the value from 180. This may seem a bit complicated, but the idea is to rotate the servo motor from 90 to 180 degrees, then 135 degrees, 90 degrees, and back to 0. This gives the illusion of rotating left and right, such as 0, 45, 90, 135, 180, 135, 90, 45, 0, 45.

To verify that this rotation effect is working, we added an angle to the serial to verify it. Finally, we added a delay of 0.2 seconds for each rotation. If you run the above code without the delay, it's easy to see why: the rotation command is issued faster than the motor is spinning, so we don't get the effect we want.

```
AutoRobot | Arduino IDE 2.3.2                                    —    □    ×
File  Edit  Sketch  Tools  Help

   ✓  →  ◐    Select Board              ▼                         ∿  ⚙

    AutoRobot.ino                                                      ...
   46
   47      // All the wheel change to stop status
   48      Robot_Stop()
   49
   50      servo.attach(ServoPin);
   51
   52      // sleep 1 second
   53      delay(1000)
   54    }
   55
   56    void loop(){
   57      int angle;
   58      if(ServoAngle > 180)
   59        angle = 180 - ServoAngle & 180;
   60      else
   61        angle = ServoAngle;
   62
   63      servo.write(angle);
   64      ServoAngle = ServoAngle + 45;
   65      if(ServoAngle >= 360 ) ServoAngle = 0;
   66      Serial.print(angle);
   67      delay(200);
   68    }

                                    Ln 52, Col 20  ✕ No board selected  ⌂
```

Ultrasonic sensors

Ultrasonic sensors take advantage of the fact that sound travels at 340 meters per second to measure distance by sending ultrasonic waves from one end and receiving the returning waves from the other, and then timing the time between the two signals. To put it another way, if you yell and shout at a mountain and then time the echo, you can get the distance.

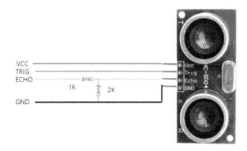

The ultrasonic sensor is supposed to have a resistor because the Echo Pin uses 3v instead of 5v. However, I used 4 220k resistors instead of 1k resistors.

We connected the Arduino in the following order: power, trigger, echo, and ground, with the trigger and echo assigned to pins 8 and 9, respectively.

```
AutoRobot | Arduino IDE 2.3.2                                    —    □    ×
File  Edit  Sketch  Tools  Help

    ⊘  →  ⊙      Select Board              ▼                        √  ⊙

      AutoRobot.ino                                                    ...
       9       * For two wheel digital input / ouput D1 to D4
      10       * D1, D2 left wheel, D3, D4 right wheel
      11       */
      12
      13     int LeftWheel_D1    =    2;
      14     int LeftWheel_D2    =    3;
      15     int RightWheel_D3   =    4;
      16     int rightWheel_D4   =    5;
      17
      18     // Servo motor pin number
      19     int ServoPin = 6;
      20     Servo servo;
      21     int ServoAngle = 90;
      22
      23     // sensor pin number for measuring distance
      24     int echoPin = 9;
      25     int trigPin = 8;
      26
      27     // if there are something in front of robot, it have to be rotate
      28     // unit : cm
      29     #define STOP_DISTANCE = 20
      30
      31     /*
                                        Ln 28, Col 13    × No board selected  ⊙
```

And, although it hasn't been used yet, we want to reorient the robot if an object is detected within 20 centimeters. Here is a routine to initialize the ultrasonic sensor inside the setup function.

```
AutoRobot | Arduino IDE 2.3.2                                    —    □    ×
File  Edit  Sketch  Tools  Help

    ⊘  →  ⊙      Select Board              ▼                        √  ⊙

      AutoRobot.ino                                                    ...
      48     // wheel pin mode define
      49     pinMod(LeftWheel_D1, OUTPUT);
      50     pinMod(LeftWheel_D2, OUTPUT);
      51     pinMod(RightWheel_D3, OUTPUT);
      52     pinMod(RightWheel_D4, OUTPUT);
      53
      54     // All the wheel change to stop status
      55     Robot_Stop()
      56
      57     servo.attach(ServoPin);
      58
      59     // sensor pin mode setup
      60     pinMode(trigPin, OUTPUT);
      61     pinMode(echoPin, INPUT)
      62
      63     // sleep 1 second
      64     delay(1000)
      65    }
      66
      67   void loop(){
      68     int angle;
      69     if(ServoAngle > 180)
      70       angle = 180 - ServoAngle & 180;
      71     else
                                        Ln 59, Col 5   × No board selected  ⊙
```

So far, all pins have been in OUTPUT mode, but the ultrasonic sensor has an incoming echo pin that needs to be set to INPUT mode. And the routine to measure the distance is a separate function, float sensor_distance(). Each call to this function returns the distance in centimeters. \

Find the distance using the formula that ultrasonic waves travel 340 meters per second.   Finally, if we call this function immediately after changing the angle of the servo motor in the loop function, we can see that the distance and angle look like this

Putting the Robot in Motion

The robot's motions can be categorized into forward, backward, left, right, and 180 degree turns. Since L298N cannot adjust the angle, we will try to adjust the angle by experience. First of all, the rotation speed also depends on the voltage of the battery, so you will have to test it yourself. The rotation of the motor itself can be changed, but we'll leave the speed as default. It's best to test with a 100% battery charge. If your battery is very worn out, it will probably spin more than it should at 100% charge.

```
void loop() {
  Robot_RightTurn();
  Robot_LeftTurn();
  Robot_180Turn();
}

/*
 * Rotate the robot 180 degrees
 */
void Robot_180Turn(){
  Serial.println("Rotate robot 180 degrees");
  digitalWrite(LeftWheel_D1, HIGH);
  digitalWrite(LeftWheel_D2, LOW);
  digitalWrite(RightWheel_D3, LOW);
  digitalWrite(RightWheel_D4, HIGH);
  delay(530);
  Robot_Stop();
  delay(250);
}

/*
 * Rotate the robot to the right
 */
void Robot_RightTurn(){
  Serial.println("Robot Right Turn");
  digitalWrite(LeftWheel_D1, LOW);
  digitalWrite(LeftWheel_D2, HIGH);
  digitalWrite(RightWheel_D3, HIGH);
  digitalWrite(RightWheel_D4, LOW);
  delay(300);
  Robot_Stop();
  delay(250);
}
```

```
/*
 * Turns the robot to the left
 */
void Robot_LeftTurn(){
  Serial.println("Robot Left Turn");
  digitalWrite(LeftWheel_D1, HIGH);
  digitalWrite(LeftWheel_D2, LOW);
  digitalWrite(RightWheel_D3, LOW);
  digitalWrite(RightWheel_D4, HIGH);
  delay(300);
  Robot_Stop();
  delay(250);
}
```

When making a right turn, only the left wheel was rotated forward while the right wheel was stopped to make a right turn. However, if the left wheel is rotated forward and the right wheel is rotated backward, it can be rotated faster, so I modified it to give forward and backward rotation for left and right turns as shown in the previous code. After executing the command and stopping it with Robot_Stop after a certain period of time, I found that about 300 meters is suitable for a 90-degree left and right rotation and 530 meters for a 180-degree rotation, so I added a function for 180-degree rotation as shown above. I wrote it as a rule of thumb. Calling Robot_Stop and again delaying it by 250 meters is in case the motor stops and starts turning in the opposite direction again. If you try to turn in the opposite direction without a delay, it will not rotate the desired angle.

Combining servo motors and ultrasonic sensors

So far, we're all set to get our robot moving. Let's check how we're going to utilize the servo motors and ultrasonic sensors. Basically, the robot needs to check for obstacles in front of it before it moves. If there are no obstacles, it moves forward and checks for obstacles again. If it encounters an obstacle, it measures the distance to the left and right. If there are obstacles in front of you and to your left and right, you can turn 180 degrees and move forward. And if either the left or right side is free of obstacles, we want to program it to turn and move forward in the direction where the obstacles are farthest away.

Here we will combine a servo motor with an ultrasonic sensor, attach the ultrasonic sensor to the servo motor, turn the servo motor in the desired direction, and measure the distance with the ultrasonic sensor. We have already tested how to utilize the servo motor and how to utilize the ultrasonic sensor.

In this section, we will create a function called Detect_Object to measure the distance to the obstacles on the right and left. The servo motor can have inputs from 0 to 179 degrees. So if we set it to 0 degrees, it will turn to the right, and if we set it to 179 degrees, it will turn to the left. Use servo.write to make it rotate. We give the rotation command and give the motor a delay of 250 milliseconds to give it enough time to rotate. Then we call a function called sensor_distance to measure the distance to an object on the right side of the robot. Using the same method, rotate the servo motor 179 degrees and measure the distance.

```
/*
 * Find the left and right distances, respectively
 */
void Detect_Object(){
  servo.write(0);
  delay(250);
  distanceRight = sensor_distance();

  servo.write(179);
  delay(250);
  distanceLeft = sensor_distance();
}

/*
 * Find the distance to the front
 */
void Detect_Front(){
  servo.write(90);
  delay(250);
  distanceFront = sensor_distance();
}
```

Detect_Object measured the distance to the left and right. Detect_Front measures the distance in front of it. The reason for the distinction between front, left, and right is that people often move forward in a straight line, and left and right are only measured when an obstacle is detected in front of them. The sensor_distance function has already been discussed earlier, so we won't describe it here.

Anomaly behavior

Earlier, when I connected the Arduino to the USB, downloaded the program, and ran it, the motor would not run even though I started the motor. This is because the power supplied to the Arduino via USB is insufficient to turn the motor. However, if you run the servo motor, the servo motor sometimes behaves abnormally. This is not only when the USB cable is plugged in, but also when using battery power. It may not rotate as much as the set value, or it may rotate at a set angle, but it may move slightly in the opposite direction, as if it is rattling. The problem with plugging the power directly into the battery is when all four wheels are spinning and the servo motors are doing the same thing. If you do a quick Google search, you'll find that some people have solved this problem by adding a capacitor. Capacitors store electricity and provide a steady supply of power during times of high power usage. You can connect the capacitor as follows to resolve the erratic behavior of the servo motor. The recommended capacitor is 25v 470uF. You can buy them for about 25 cents if you search online. Connect the battery on the left and the servo motor

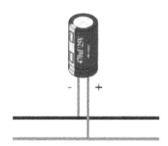

However, I didn't have any capacitors on hand, so I connected two 220uF as shown in the following photo.

The next thing is that the ultrasonic sensor sometimes sends weird readings, but once the power supply stabilized, I didn't see any significant spikes, so I left it alone. However, if this is an issue for you, you can try using a separate library called NewPing by visiting the following website.

https://www.makerguides.com/hc-sr04-arduino-tutorial/

Autopilot algorithms

Once powered up, the robot avoids obstacles and keeps moving until its battery runs out. The information we have depends on the information coming from the ultrasonic sensor. So, we wrote the loop function as follows. As we mentioned at the beginning, a loop function is a function that repeats infinitely. The infinitely looping function is the function in the next 20 lines, and it's what keeps the robot moving and avoiding obstacles.

```
void loop() {
  Detect_Front(); // Measuring frontal distance
  // Move forward and check for objects if greater than a defined distance
  if(distanceFront > STOP_DISTANCE)
  {
    Robot_Go();
  } else {            // If the distance of the front is less than the defined distance
    Detect_Object();    // Find the distance to the left and right
    // If both are less than the specified distance
    if (distanceRight < STOP_DISTANCE && distanceLeft < STOP_DISTANCE){
      Robot_180Turn();  // Rotate 180 degrees
    } else {
      if(distanceRight >= distanceLeft) // If the distance to the right is greater
        Robot_RightTurn();         // Turn right
      else                    // If the distance to the left is greater
        Robot_LeftTurn();          // Turn left
    }
  }
}
```

Detect_Front();

It's not a complicated algorithm, but I'll try to explain it in writing. At the beginning of the loop, we first measure the distance to the obstacle in front of us using the Detect_Front function.

if(distanceFront > STOP_DISTANCE)

Detect_Front() measures the distance and stores it in a variable called distanceFront. It compares this variable to the STOP_DISTANCE we specified. It would be correct to return the return value of the Detect_Front function as the measured distance, and distanceFront should receive the return value, but the Detect_Object() function that will appear next has two variables, each with a measurement value, so we need to implement it as a structure or class, which may be difficult for beginners to understand, so we use a global variable.   If the measured distance is greater than STOP_DISTANCE, then execute Robot_Go() in the following {...}. Then we move to the end of the function without executing the else statement. If the measured distance is less than or equal to STOP_DISTANCE, then the else statement is executed.   Assuming that this if statement is always true, the robot will continue to move forward as the measured distance decreases. The Robot_Go() function advances 300 meters and calls Robot_Stop(). Next, it moves to the front of the loop and calls Detect_Front() to measure the distance to the object in front of it. Because we rotated the servo motor 90 degrees to the front and gave it a 250-millisecond delay when measuring the object, and used 20 milliseconds to measure the distance, the robot's behavior will be 300 milliseconds of travel and 270 milliseconds of standing.

else Statement

The following is an else statement that occurs when the measured value is less than STOP_DISTANCE. Encountering this statement means that the robot has no room to move forward. So it has three choices: turn right, turn left, or make a U-turn.   The first part of the else statement calls the Detect_Object() function, which measures the distance to the left and right, and gets the distance values for distanceRight and distanceLeft. The servo motor measures the distance as it moves left and right.   After the measurements are made, there is an if ~ else ~ statement.

if (distanceRight < STOP DISTANCE && distanceLeft < STOP DISTANCE)

The distance to the left and right are both closer than the specified distance, but there is an object, so there is no room to move to the front, left, and right. Therefore, we use the 180-degree turn function Robot_180Turn() to make a U-turn and move to the end of the function. Since it is an infinite loop, when we move to the front of the loop, we measure the distance to the object in front of us again. We measure the distance because the object that was in the back before Robot_180Turn() is in the front again after the turn.

else Statement

This is true if at least one of the spaces on the left and right is farther away than STOP_DISTANCE. They can both be farther than STOP_DISTANCE, or only one of them can be farther than STOP_DISTANCE. In any case, one of them is farther than the STOP_DISTANCE. Here we compare distanceRight and distanceLeft, and if distanceRight is greater than or equal to distanceLeft, we turn right (Robot_RightTurn()), if less, we turn left (Robot_LeftTurn()), and move to the end of the function.

The end result

Here's the code we've seen so far. This is not a lot of code for a self-driving robot. Let's take a look at what we've done so far and see what's missing.

```
/*******************************************************
 *          AutoRobot
 *                    made by Sohyemini
 *                    2024.04.02
 *******************************************************/
#include <Servo.h>
/*
 * Declare digital inputs/outputs D1 through D4 for two wheels
 * D1, D2 are left wheels, D3, D4 are right wheels
 */
int LeftWheel_D1  =  2;
int LeftWheel_D2  =  3;
int RightWheel_D3 =  4;
int RightWheel_D4 =  5;

// Servo motor pin number for moving the ultrasonic sensor
int ServoPin = 6;
Servo servo;

// Variables to store object distances in front, left, and right
float distanceFront;
float distanceLeft;
float distanceRight;

// Pin number of each ultrasonic sensor, for distance measurement
int echoPin = 9;
int trigPin = 8;

// If an obstacle enters this range, you must turn around
// Units are centimeters
#define STOP_DISTANCE 40
 /*
  * Declare the function responsible for moving the robot and declare the delay
  */
void Robot_Stop();
void Robot_Go();
void Robot_RightTurn();
void Robot_LeftTurn();
void Robot_180Turn();
```

```
void Detect_Front();
void Detect_Object();
/*
 * Start Arduino with an initialization function and run it only once
 */
void setup() {
  // Initialize Serial to view debugging messages
  Serial.begin(115200);
  Serial.println("");
  // Defines the pin mode of the wheel
  pinMode(LeftWheel_D1, OUTPUT);
  pinMode(LeftWheel_D2, OUTPUT);
  pinMode(RightWheel_D3, OUTPUT);
  pinMode(RightWheel_D4, OUTPUT);

  // Reset all wheels to a stationary state
  Robot_Stop();
  // Initializing Servo Motors
  servo.attach(ServoPin);
  servo.write(90); // Set to face forward

  // Setting the Pin Mode for Ultrasonic Sensors
  pinMode(trigPin, OUTPUT);
  pinMode(echoPin, INPUT);
  //1 second pause
  delay(1000);
}

void loop() {
  Detect_Front(); // Measuring frontal distance
  // Move forward and check for objects if greater than a defined distance
  if(distanceFront > STOP_DISTANCE)
  {
    Robot_Go();
  } else {          // If the distance of the front is less than the defined distance
    Detect_Object();   // Find the distance to the left and right
    // If both are less than the specified distance
    if (distanceRight < STOP_DISTANCE && distanceLeft < STOP_DISTANCE){
      Robot_180Turn(); // Rotate 180 degrees
    }
    else {

      if(distanceRight >= distanceLeft) // If the distance to the right is greater
      Robot_RightTurn();          // Turn right
      else                 // If the distance to the left is greater
      Robot_LeftTurn();          // Turn left
    }
  }
}
```

```
/*
 * Rotate the robot 180 degrees
 */
void Robot_180Turn(){
  Serial.println("Rotate robot 180 degrees");
  digitalWrite(LeftWheel_D1, HIGH);
  digitalWrite(LeftWheel_D2, LOW);
  digitalWrite(RightWheel_D3, LOW);
  digitalWrite(RightWheel_D4, HIGH);
  delay(530);
  Robot_Stop();
  delay(250);
}

/*
 * Rotate the robot to the right
 */
void Robot_RightTurn(){
  Serial.println("Robot Right Turn");
  digitalWrite(LeftWheel_D1, LOW);
  digitalWrite(LeftWheel_D2, HIGH);
  digitalWrite(RightWheel_D3, HIGH);
  digitalWrite(RightWheel_D4, LOW);
  delay(300);
  Robot_Stop();
  delay(250);
}

/*
 * Rotate the bot to the left
 */
void Robot_LeftTurn(){
  Serial.println("Robot Left Turn");
  digitalWrite(LeftWheel_D1, HIGH);
  digitalWrite(LeftWheel_D2, LOW);
  digitalWrite(RightWheel_D3, LOW);
  digitalWrite(RightWheel_D4, HIGH);
  delay(300);
  Robot_Stop();
  delay(250);
}

/*
 * Stop the robot
 */
void Robot_Stop(){
  Serial.println("Stop the robot");
  digitalWrite(LeftWheel_D1, HIGH);
  digitalWrite(LeftWheel_D2, HIGH);
```

```
    digitalWrite(RightWheel_D3, HIGH);
    digitalWrite(RightWheel_D4, HIGH);
}

/*
 * The robot moves forward
 */
void Robot_Go(){
  Serial.println("Robot Advancement");
  digitalWrite(LeftWheel_D1, HIGH);
  digitalWrite(LeftWheel_D2, LOW);
  digitalWrite(RightWheel_D3, HIGH);
  digitalWrite(RightWheel_D4, LOW);
  delay(300);
  Robot_Stop();
}


/*
 * Move the robot backward
 */
void Robot_Back(){
  Serial.println("Robot reversing");
  digitalWrite(LeftWheel_D1, LOW);
  digitalWrite(LeftWheel_D2, HIGH);
  digitalWrite(RightWheel_D3, LOW);
  digitalWrite(RightWheel_D4, HIGH);
}

/*
 * Function to find the distance of an ultrasonic sensor
 */
float sensor_distance() {
  float distance = 0;

  // Use the trigger pin to emit ultrasound and go into standby mode
  digitalWrite(trigPin, HIGH);
  delayMicroseconds(20);
  digitalWrite(trigPin, LOW);

  // The time the ultrasound came in, in microseconds
  // It travels 340 meters per second, which is microseconds here, and
  // This is the round trip distance, so we divide by 2.
  // It's complicated, so we can divide by 58.5.
  distance = pulseIn(echoPin, HIGH) / 58.8;
  return distance;
}
```

```
/*
 * Find the left and right distances, respectively
 */
void Detect_Object(){
  servo.write(0);
  delay(250);
  distanceRight = sensor_distance();

  servo.write(179);
  delay(250);
  distanceLeft = sensor_distance();
}

/*
 * Find the distance to the front
 */
void Detect_Front(){
  servo.write(90);
  delay(250);
  distanceFront = sensor_distance();
}
```

The downside

If you've driven your robot a few times, you've probably noticed that there are a lot of things that are frustrating. First of all, it doesn't look good when it stops in the middle of a run. Secondly, the turning angle is not accurate and varies slightly from one maneuver to the next. I would like it to move faster when there is an obstacle far ahead and then slow down when it gets closer. Most importantly, the ultrasonic sensor has a range problem, which means that the robot tries to keep moving forward even when there are floors or thin objects that it can't detect, and it frequently collides with objects because the ultrasonic sensor's measurements are inaccurate. Due to the limitations of the servo motor, it takes quite a while to measure the distance. A solution to this problem could be to install multiple ultrasonic sensors. In fact, while surfing the web, I found an Arduino RC Car with multiple ultrasonic sensors.

https://www.tindie.com/products/arielnh56/octosonarx2-connect-16-x-hc-sr04-to-arduino/

The speed of the motor can be set to L298N. To implement this, it is necessary to have several ultrasonic sensors to measure the distance to the obstacle in a short time. To control the speed using the L298N, there is an Enable jumper on the left and right side of D1 to D4. A jumper is a pin that has two pins instead of one, as shown in D1 through D4, that can be connected or shorted to set some information. The jumper to the left of D1 is connected, which means that the left motor is enabled. The right motor is similarly enabled.

You can adjust the speed by removing the jumper in the red part of the image and connecting the lower of the two pins to the Arduino's digital input and outputting a value between 0 and 255. 255 is full speed and 0 is stop. This pin is called PWM, which stands for Pulse Width Modulation. And to get it to move at the correct angle, you'll need to use a stepper motor, or what we used, a DC motor with something called an encoder. Thin objects may not be easy to detect, but the problem of how to detect objects on the ground, objects that the robot's wheels can't move because they get stuck, can be solved by using infrared sensors. Infrared sensors can typically measure distances of up to 30 centimeters, so it would be useful to install them on the bottom of the robot and use them to measure distances. The infrared sensor called SZH-SSBH-002 is said to be able to measure from 2 to 30 centimeters, and the distance can be set by adjusting the variable resistor on the board. And it doesn't receive a distance value, but if there is an object at the distance set by the rheostat, the connected pin goes HIGH, otherwise it goes LOW. It's a very basic sensor.

We want to mount this sensor on the front lower part of the robot and set it to detect if there are any obstacles in the front lower part that the ultrasonic sensor cannot detect at the beginning of every loop function.

Step 3. Upgrade

When I first built my autonomous robot, I listed my regrets. There were quite a few instances where the robot failed to detect obstacles due to sensor limitations and didn't move as expected. If I started the robot in the living room, it would drive back and forth for a while and then end up in the kitchen or somewhere in the kid's room. So I ordered a few upgrades.

- Bluetooth Module (HC-06)
- Infrared Distance Measurement Module (HS-IRSM)
- LCD Module

SZH-SSBH-002 Sensor

I ordered the Bluetooth module because I thought it would be interesting to manually control the car rather than autonomous driving. In fact, I tested it with the remote control module first, but I accidentally shorted out the remote control input (IR) and burned it, but a big part of the reason was that the IR input can only be input from the front of the receiver. This is easy to understand if you think of a TV remote control. The remote works well in front of the TV, but not behind the TV. Bluetooth, on the other hand, can transmit and receive data up to about 10 meters, so it seemed like a good choice for a wireless remote control. I checked around and found several Arduino control applications for smartphones. I decided not to create my own application for the smartphone, but to use what others have created. Next up is the infrared ranging module. These modules are inexpensive and only return a digital pin indicating whether there is a distance or not, i.e. "there is an obstacle" or "there is no obstacle", but not how far away. So there is a rheostat on the board that allows you to change the distance. You have to set it by turning it with a Phillips screwdriver and testing the desired distance. The sensor can determine the presence of obstacles up to 30 centimeters away. When the red LED on the board gets brighter, an obstacle is detected. We want to attach it to the bottom of the robot and use it to compensate for errors in the ultrasonic sensor's distance measurements. We want to use an ultrasonic sensor on the top of the robot and a module that uses infrared light on the bottom.

Finally, we have the LCD module. It's not really necessary for an autonomous robot, but I thought it would be nice to display the current mode and print out the car's behavior. The LCD can only display two lines and can output 16 characters each. Also, I know that Korean characters cannot be output.

Bluetooth Module

The HC-06 looks like this and has RX and TX lines in addition to VCC and GND. RX is the pin for receiving signals and TX is the pin for transmitting data. In total, there are four pins to connect.

 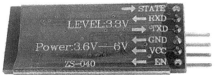

Note that RX and TX are the pins that receive and send signals respectively, so the RX of the Arduino board must be connected to the TX of the HC-06 and the TX to the RX.

Serial communication

Before we talk about Bluetooth, let's talk about serial communication, because that's what we're going to use it for. Serial communication translates to serial communication. In general, we're talking about sending data in a single direction using one or two wires. There are various standards for serial communication, but the method we will use here uses two lines, RX and TX, as described above, except for VCC and GND for power. Since it is said that data is transmitted in a single direction, from the HC-06 Bluetooth board's point of view, RX, which reads data, performs a single communication that only receives data, and TX, which sends data, is in charge of only sending function. Therefore, it only receives on one side and sends on one side. When sending and receiving data, we use 0 and 1 to send and receive one bit each. Since each character is composed of 8 bits, you need to send 8 bits of data in sequence to send one character. In addition, you have the option to send additional information, such as whether the data was delivered correctly. So it takes more data transfers to send a single character. And the speeds of the receiver and sender must be exactly matched in order to send and receive information.

Initialize Bluetooth

Since Bluetooth uses serial communication, we will use the software library module defined as SoftwareSerial. You can add the header file to the top of the source code by hand, such as #include <SoftwareSerial.h>, or you can select SoftwareSerial from Sketch → Include Libraries and it will automatically add the header file to the source code.

Next, we need to connect the RX and TX of the HC-06 board to the pins of the Arduino for serial communication. It is important to note that RX, which reads data from the HC-06 board, must be connected to TX, which is the signal sent by the Arduino board. Conversely, the TX must be connected to the RX of the Arduino to function properly. Please be careful when making this connection.

So we declared BT as SoftwareSerial and assigned RX and TX to 10 and 11 respectively. We can connect pin 10 to the TX of the HC-06 and pin 11 to the RX.

```
#include <SoftwareSerial.h>

//Bluetooth setup
SoftwareSerial BT(10,11);  //rx, tx

// Do you want to use the remote or let the car drive itself?
// Default is to use the remote

bool  Auto_Drive = false;

void setup() {
  // Initialize Serial to view debugging messages
  Serial.begin(9600);
  //Serial.println("");
  while(!Serial);

  BT.begin(9600);
}
```

Until now, it only operated in autonomous mode using the ultrasonic sensor after powering up. However, I want to add a mode that uses Bluetooth for autonomous driving and a mode that users can manually operate using a Bluetooth app on their smartphone. So I created a variable called Auto_Drive to specify whether the current driving mode is autonomous or manual. I set it to false at startup, so when the power is turned on, it will start in manual mode. Next, in the setup function, we set the BT speed to 9600 baud. This means that the Arduino and HC-06 will communicate at a baud rate of 9600. 9600 means 9600 bits per second, which means that 9600 bits can be sent in one second.

AT commands

The AT command is a language that WinRAR used to control modems and is now standard for all communications. The HC-06 can also be controlled through this command. First, code the following at the top of the loop function. This is to check communication with the Bluetooth module, assuming the pins are connected properly. The first if statement in the code is to output what is being typed into the BT in the serial communication window when BT is available. The second if statement tells the Bluetooth BT to send whatever is typed into the Serial input window when the Serial is available, whether it is for debug purposes or not.

```
void loop() {
  if (BT.available()) {
    Serial.write(BT.read());
  }
  if (Serial.available()) {
    BT.write(Serial.read());
  }
  return;
  .
  .
  .
}
```

When you're done coding, press Upload in the sketch to compile and upload the binary. And then download and open the serial monitor. At the bottom, change both NL & CR and the speed to 9600 baud.

Now we're ready to communicate with our computer and Arduino using Bluetooth, and once that's established, let's try to connect to our smartphone.

First, type AT into the input box on the serial screen and you should see OK below. If you send the command AT to the Bluetooth, you should get an OK reply from the HC-06. If you don't get an OK, there's a problem with the connection or setting of the pin. You can try typing AT+NAME? to see the name of your BT, and finally, you can try typing AT+PIN? to see the password, as it's set by default. To rename it to your liking, just type AT+NAME followed by your name. To change it to HYEMIN, type AT+NAMEHYEMIN. The same goes for your password. You can type something like AT+PIN7777. One thing that baffles me is that there are so many BT modules, and I don't know if it's because of version differences, but the AT commands I got from Googling often don't work. Also, make sure to match both NL & CR and board rate as shown in the bottom part of the following picture.

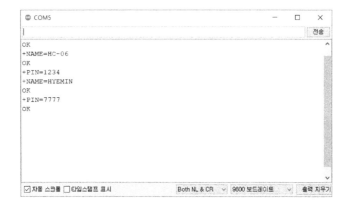

Connect your smartphone to your Arduino

Go to your smartphone's application market and search for "arduino bluetooth" to download the arduino bluetooth controller.

This is the result of searching the Android App Market, from left to right, and this is the result of searching for the device by pressing the magnifying glass button while the robot is powered on after completing the installation. Here we see the device with the name we specified. It looks weird with a number after it, but the device name is displayed correctly in the part where you enter the password. If the password is correct, it will ask you what mode you want to start in, as shown on the far left of the second line above. If you select Controller mode at the top, it will look like the second image below. Since we haven't set up the Controller, we need to press the settings button in the upper right corner and press each of the settings as shown in the far right image below. You can then control the robot using the directional buttons and switch to manual mode. Assign the keys as follows.

Assign d for forward, e for backward, b for left, and c for right, and then assign a for stop, a for the triangle, o for manual mode, and p for autonomous driving.   Once you're done, press the buttons on the smartphone controller one by one and check that the characters d,e,b,c,a,o,p are displayed on the serial screen connected to the Arduino. We'll use these characters to control the robot's driving.

Manual control of robots

Here is the code for controlling the robot. First of all, the previous code that sends and receives data is commented out, but you can delete it since we have already tested it all.

The important part here is the variable called Auto_Drive. We declared Auto_Drive as false, so it's a manual driving mode. If this variable changes to true, it will change to autonomous driving mode. So basically, the loop function is divided into two parts depending on whether it's autonomous or manual driving.

In manual mode, we use the BT.read() function to find out what command came in. The switch statement is new to us, but you can easily see that we've written a bunch of if statements. Depending on the conditions in the parentheses of the switch() statement, we move to the appropriate case. We do everything below the case, and when we encounter the break statement, we move to the end of the switch statement.

For example, when the character a comes in, it prints "Stop Btn" to the serial window, stops using Robot_Stop, and ends. I'm sure the code related to the robot's movement will be easy to understand, you've seen these functions before. However, when manual mode o and autonomous mode p come in, it changes the variable called Auto_Drive, so the next time you enter the loop function, you can determine whether it is autonomous or manual driving by looking at the changed Auto_Drive variable.

The else statement is the self-driving mode. In autonomous mode, everything is ignored except a command to change to manual mode, so we have an if statement to check if the manual mode command 'o' comes in. If the command to switch to manual mode comes in, we stop the robot and change Auto_Drive to false to switch to manual mode. Then the next time the loop starts, it will be in manual mode.

```
Void loop() {
/*
  if (BT.available()) {
    Serial.write(BT.read());
  }
  if (Serial.available()) {
    BT.write(Serial.read());
  }
  return;
*/

  if(!Auto_Drive)
  {
    switch(BT.read())
    {
      case 'a':
        Serial.println("Stop Btn");
        Robot_Stop();
        break;
      case 'b':
        Serial.println("Right Btn");
        Robot_RightTurn();
        break;
      case 'c':
        Serial.println("Left Btn");
        Robot_LeftTurn();
        break;
      case 'd':
        Serial.println("Go Btn");
        Robot_Go();
        break;
      case 'e':
        Serial.println("Back Btn");
        Robot_Back();
        break;
      case 'o':
        Serial.println("o Btn / Manual Mode");
        Auto_Drive = false;
        break;
      case 'p':
        Serial.println("p Btn / Auto Mode");
        Robot_Stop();
        Detect_Object();
        Auto_Drive = true;
        break;
    }
  } else {
```

```
if('o' == BT.read()){
    Serial.println("o Btn / Manual Mode");
    Auto_Drive = false;
    Robot_Stop();
    return;
}
//Existing autonomous driving code
.
.
.
{
}
```

Once you've finalized the coding, let's try driving the robot. After the program is downloaded via USB, the robot doesn't do anything because it's in manual mode. Now, if you connect the Bluetooth from your smartphone and enter controller mode, you can manually move the robot or change it to automatic driving mode. But there's one strange behavior. When I press forward, it moves forward a little bit and then stops. This is not fun to drive because you don't need a stop button. So I made the following changes to the Robot_Go() function.

```
void Robot_Go(){
  Serial.println("Robot Advancement");
  digitalWrite(LeftWheel_D1, HIGH);
  digitalWrite(LeftWheel_D2, LOW);
  digitalWrite(RightWheel_D3, HIGH);
  digitalWrite(RightWheel_D4, LOW);
  if(Auto_Drive)
  {
    delay(300);
    Robot_Stop();
  }
}
```

Do you understand what this means? The if statement has been added. What it means is that only when in autonomous mode should the robot be driven for 300 pre-seconds before stopping. This means that in manual mode, if you press the forward button once, it will continue to move forward until another button is pressed.

Connecting power to additional modules

Due to the sensors we used before using Bluetooth, we used all the power pins from the Arduino to each sensor. Therefore, we had to use the L298N's 5v out instead of connecting the power from Bluetooth directly to the Arduino. I only used the 12v input and the GND next to it, but I used the 5V output on the far right. And only the data line is connected to the Arduino.

As shown in the previous figure, the 298N's power supply has a 7v input, GND, and a third 5v output with multiple power lines going to each module and sensor.

Infrared Distance Measurement Module (HS-IRSM)

The infrared distance measurement module looks like this. The pin connections connect one data line to the Arduino and one to power.

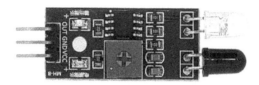

It has two LEDs that emit infrared light from one side and receive it from the other. The ultrasonic sensors we've used so far are sound waves, but we can't hear them, and we can't see infrared light because it's out of the visible light region where we can see. However, in the case of infrared, we can see it with a digital camera. The following photo was taken with the module mounted on the bottom front of the robot and powered on. You can see light coming out of one of the LEDs that was transparent. If you are using infrared light like this, you can use a camera to see if it is emitting infrared light. Since the remote control uses a lot of infrared light, you can check if it is emitting infrared light by looking at the front of the TV remote control with your phone's camera.

The code looks like this. The code is self-explanatory, so you should be able to understand it without much explanation. The input is received on pin 7 and the pin is set to input mode because it is to receive and read the value from the sensor. The digitalRead function is used to read the value and output 0 or 1.

```
// The infrared obstacle detection sensor is set to digital pin 7.
int infrared  = 7;

void setup(){
  // Set the infrared obstacle detection sensor pin to INPUT.
  pinMode(infrared, INPUT);
}

void loop(){
  // Reads sensor values starting with the infrared sensor.


  // It will return 0 if detected and 1 if not detected.
  int state = digitalRead(infrared);

  // Output the measured sensor values to the serial monitor.
  Serial.print("Infrared = ");
  Serial.println(state);
}
```

Since the sensor is mounted on the bottom of the robot as shown in the previous photo, it will output 0 if the robot detects an object in the lower part of the robot, and if it receives 0, there is an obstacle in front of the robot, so we can change it to drive around it. Code as before and bring the obstacle light near the sensor to see at what distance the value changes to 0 to detect an obstacle. Check the distance and adjust the rheostat on the sensor to detect the object at the right distance.

Place the object at a reasonable distance, rotate the rheostat, and watch the serial window to confirm the distance.

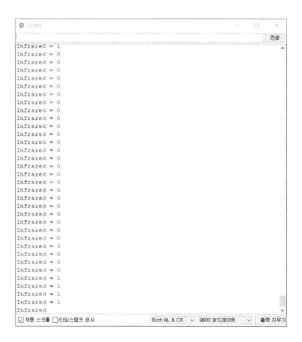

There is a way to check if an object is detected without the serial window. If the red LED on the module glows brighter, an object has been detected.

```
void loop(){
 // Read the sensor values starting with the infrared sensor.
 // 0 if detected, 1 if not detected.
 int state = digitalRead(infrared);
 if(state == 0)
 {
  Robot_Back();
  delay(200);
  Robot_180Turn();
  return;
 }

 // Existing code
}
```

After the distance was specified, the code looked like the previous one. When an object is detected, the robot backs up for 200 milliseconds and then makes a 180-degree turn. The loop function ends with a return. The next time the loop function is executed, the robot will use the ultrasonic sensor to check for an object in front of it, and the robot will continue to drive autonomously depending on the situation.

LCD Module

The LCD module was chosen because it has nothing to do with the robot's driving performance, but it can display information about the vehicle's status and is not difficult to implement. We used a 1602 Character LCD, which is an inexpensive LCD that can display 16 characters on two lines.

As you can see in the previous photo, there are quite a few pins to connect. Since we have only a few digital pins left, we can't connect them right now. However, we can solve the problem by using the I2C LCD Interface.

We need to add a library. This is because we will be using an already created library. In your development environment, select Tools → Manage Libraries to install LiquidCrystal I2C.

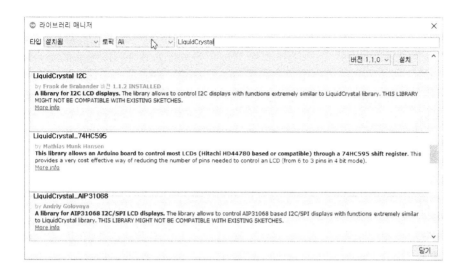

What is I2C?

It is also called IIC and is pronounced I-SQUARE-C. It stands for inter-Intergrated Circuit and is a bidirectional two-wire serial bus. You can compare it to serial communication from earlier. It uses two wires, one for timing synchronization and one for data, and can connect up to 127 peripherals.

The I2C LCD module has two pins besides GND and VCC. These two pins are used to send information from the Arduino to the LCD. If you buy an LCD module and an I2C LCD module, it is easy to plug them in in the right direction, but I bought both modules with only the pins listed, so I used a universal board to make the following connections.

The dip switch opposite the pin on the I2C module turns the LCD backlight on when plugged in and off when unplugged. And while it's on, the brightness can be adjusted using a variable resistor right after the pin. I initially set the brightness too high and thought that the characters wouldn't be displayed, so after connecting the Arduino and L298N to power, I adjusted the brightness accordingly and tested it.

```
#include <Wire.h>
#include <LiquidCrystal_I2C.h>

void setup(){
  // Initialize Serial to view debugging messages
  Serial.begin(9600);
  //Serial.println("");
  while(!Serial);

  Wire.begin();
}
```

```
void loop(){
  byte error, address;
  int nDevices;
  Serial.println("Scanning...");
  nDevices = 0;
  for(address = 1; address < 127; address++ )
  {
    Wire.beginTransmission(address);
    error = Wire.endTransmission();

    if (error == 0)
    {
      Serial.print("I2C device found at address 0x");

      if (address<16)
        Serial.print("0");
      Serial.print(address,HEX);
      Serial.println("  !");

      nDevices++;
    }
    else if (error==4)
    {
      Serial.print("Unknow error at address 0x");
      if (address<16)
        Serial.print("0");
      Serial.println(address,HEX);
    }
  }
  if (nDevices == 0)
    Serial.println("No I2C devices found\n");
  else
    Serial.println("done\n");

  delay(5000);

  return;

  // Existing code=
  .
  .
  .
}
```

The previous code looks complicated, but it is a temporary code to get the address of the I2C LCD module needed for I2C communication. Let's use this code to get the address. The address will appear in the Serial window.

```
#include <Servo.h>
#include <SoftwareSerial.h>
#include <Wire.h>
#include <LiquidCrystal_I2C.h>

// Create a 16x2 LCD object with an I2C address of 0x27
// (the I2C address will need to be modified to match your LCD).


LiquidCrystal_I2C lcd(0x27, 16, 2);

void setup() {
  // Initialize Serial to view debugging messages
  Serial.begin(9600);
  //Serial.println("");
  while(!Serial);
  BT.begin(9600);

  //Wire.begin();

  // Initialize the I2C LCD...
  lcd.init();
  // Turns on the backlight of the I2C LCD.
  lcd.backlight();
}

void loop(){
  .
  .

  .
  if(!Auto_Drive)
  {
    printLCD1("Manual mode");
    switch(BT.read())
    {
      case 'a':
        Serial.println("Stop Btn");
        printLCD2("Stop");
        Robot_Stop();
        break;

  .
  .
  .
}
```

Delete the code inside the existing loop function and add the lcd to the setup. Then use the printLCD1,2 function to print the message on the first and second lines. That's all there is to it: setCursor to position it and print it out.

```
void printLCD1(String str){
    // Have them start in cell 0 of line 0.
    lcd.setCursor(0,0);
    // Print the sentence below.
    lcd.print(str);
}

void printLCD2(String str){
    // Have them start in cell 0 of line 1.
    lcd.setCursor(0,1);
    // Print the sentence below.
    lcd.print(str);
}
```

Step 4. Final Code

So far, we've been working together to build a robot that can drive autonomously using an Arduino. In this chapter, you'll see the full source code. I encourage you to look at your code and mine to see how they work together, and to watch them in action. If you have a better idea, don't hesitate to modify it and make it work better.

```
/*****************************************************
 *            AutoRobot
 *                      made by Sohyemini
 *                      2024.04.02
 *****************************************************/
#include <Servo.h>
#include <SoftwareSerial.h>
#include <Wire.h>
#include <LiquidCrystal_I2C.h>

/*
 * Declare digital inputs/outputs D1 through D4 for the two wheels.
 * D1, D2 are the left wheels, D3, D4 are the right wheels
 */
int LeftWheel_D1  =  2;
int LeftWheel_D2  =  3;
int RightWheel_D3 =  4;
int RightWheel_D4 =  5;

// Servo motor pin number to move the ultrasonic sensor
int ServoPin = 6;
Servo servo;

// Set the infrared obstacle detection sensor to digital pin 7.
int infrared  = 7;

// A variable to store distances of objects in front, left, and right
float distanceFront;
```

```
float distanceLeft;
float distanceRight;

// pin number of each ultrasonic sensor, for distance measurement
int echoPin = 9;
int trigPin = 8;

// If an obstacle enters this range, it must be turned around
// The unit is centimeters

#define STOP_DISTANCE 40

//Bluetooth setup
SoftwareSerial BT(10,11);  //rx, tx

// Do you want to use the remote or let the car drive itself?
// Default is to use the rem

bool  Auto_Drive = false;

// Create a 16x2 LCD object with an I2C address of 0x27
// (the I2C address will need to be modified to match your LCD).
LiquidCrystal_I2C lcd(0x27, 16, 2);

/*
 * Declare the function responsible for moving the robot and declare the delay
 */

void Robot_Stop();
void Robot_Go();
void Robot_RightTurn();
void Robot_LeftTurn();
void Robot_180Turn();
void Robot_Back();

void Detect_Front();
void Detect_Object();

void I2C_Address_Check(); // Check the I2C_Address

void printLCD1(String str);
void printLCD2(String str);
/*
```

```
 * Start Arduino with an initialization function and run only once
 */
void setup() {
  // Initialize Serial to view debugging messages
  Serial.begin(9600);
  //Serial.println("");
  while(!Serial);
  BT.begin(9600);

  // Defines the pin mode of the wheel
  pinMode(LeftWheel_D1, OUTPUT);
  pinMode(LeftWheel_D2, OUTPUT);
  pinMode(RightWheel_D3, OUTPUT);
  pinMode(RightWheel_D4, OUTPUT);

  // reset all wheels to a stationary state
  Robot_Stop();

  // Initialize servo motor
  servo.attach(ServoPin);
  servo.write(90); // Set to face forward

  // Set the pin mode of the ultrasonic sensor
  pinMode(trigPin, OUTPUT);
  pinMode(echoPin, INPUT);

  // Set the infrared obstacle detection sensor pin to INPUT.
  pinMode(infrared, INPUT);

  //Wire.begin();

  // Initialize the I2C LCD...
  lcd.init();
  // Turns on the backlight of the I2C LCD.
  lcd.backlight();

  //1 second pause
  delay(1000);
  Detect_Front();
}

void loop() {
  I2C_Address_Check(); // I2C address check
```

```
/*
if (BT.available()) {
  Serial.write(BT.read());
}
if (Serial.available()) {
  BT.write(Serial.read());
}
*/

// Read the sensor values starting with the infrared sensor.
// 0 if detected, 1 if not detected.

int state = digitalRead(infrared);
if(state == 0)
{
  Robot_Back();
  delay(200);
  Robot_180Turn();
  return;
}
// Output the measured sensor value to the serial monitor.
/*
Serial.print("Infrared = ");
Serial.println(state);
*/

if(!Auto_Drive)
{
  printLCD1("Manual mode");
  switch(BT.read())
  {
    case 'a':
      Serial.println("Stop Btn");
      printLCD2("Stop");
      Robot_Stop();
      break;
    case 'b':
      Serial.println("Right Btn");
      printLCD2("Turn Right");
      Robot_RightTurn();
      break;
    case 'c':
      Serial.println("Left Btn");
      printLCD2("Turn Left");
      Robot_LeftTurn();
```

```
      break;
   case 'd':
      Serial.println("Go Btn");
      printLCD2("Go Go ...");
      Robot_Go();
      break;
   case 'e':
      Serial.println("Back Btn");
      printLCD2("Back ...");
      Robot_Back();
      break;
   case 'o':
      Serial.println("# Btn / Manual mode");
      Auto_Drive = false;
      break;
   case 'p':
      Serial.println("* Btn / Auto Mode");
      Robot_Stop();
      Detect_Object();
      Auto_Drive = true;
      break;
   }
 } else {
   printLCD1("Auto Drive Mode");
   printLCD2("Made by SoHyeMin");
    if('o' == BT.read()){
      Serial.println("# Btn / Manual Mode");
      Auto_Drive = false;
      Robot_Stop();
      return;
    }
  // Autonomous Mode
  // If greater than a defined distance, move forward and check for objects
  if(distanceFront > STOP_DISTANCE)
  {
    Robot_Go();
  } else {         // if the distance of the front is less than the defined distance
    Detect_Object();    // Find the distance between left and right
    // If both are less than the specified distance
    if (distanceRight < STOP_DISTANCE && distanceLeft < STOP_DISTANCE){
      Robot_180Turn();  // Rotate 180 degrees
    }
    else {
      if(distanceRight >= distanceLeft) // If the distance to the right is greater
        Robot_RightTurn();           // Turn right
```

```
      else                    // If the distance to the left is greater
        Robot_LeftTurn();        // Turn left
      }
    }
    Detect_Front(); // Measuring frontal distance
  }
}

/*
 * Rotate the robot 180 degrees
 */
void Robot_180Turn(){
  Serial.println("Rotate robot 180 degrees");
  digitalWrite(LeftWheel_D1, HIGH);
  digitalWrite(LeftWheel_D2, LOW);
  digitalWrite(RightWheel_D3, LOW);
  digitalWrite(RightWheel_D4, HIGH);
  delay(530);
  Robot_Stop();
  delay(250);
}

/*
 * Rotate the robot to the right
 */
void Robot_RightTurn(){
  Serial.println("Robot Right Turn");
  digitalWrite(LeftWheel_D1, HIGH);
  digitalWrite(LeftWheel_D2, HIGH);
  digitalWrite(RightWheel_D3, HIGH);
  digitalWrite(RightWheel_D4, LOW);
  //if(Auto_Drive)
  {
    delay(300);
    Robot_Stop();
    delay(250);
  }
}

/*
 * Rotate the robot to the left
 */
void Robot_LeftTurn(){
  Serial.println("Robot Left Turn");
  digitalWrite(LeftWheel_D1, HIGH);
```

```
  digitalWrite(LeftWheel_D2, LOW);
  digitalWrite(RightWheel_D3, HIGH);
  digitalWrite(RightWheel_D4, HIGH);
  //if(Auto_Drive)
  {
    delay(300);
    Robot_Stop();
    delay(250);
  }
}

/*
 * Stop the robot
 */
void Robot_Stop(){
  Serial.println("Stop the robot");
  digitalWrite(LeftWheel_D1, HIGH);
  digitalWrite(LeftWheel_D2, HIGH);
  digitalWrite(RightWheel_D3, HIGH);
  digitalWrite(RightWheel_D4, HIGH);
}

/*
 * The robot moves forward
 */
void Robot_Go(){
  Serial.println("Robot Advancement");
  digitalWrite(LeftWheel_D1, HIGH);
  digitalWrite(LeftWheel_D2, LOW);
  digitalWrite(RightWheel_D3, HIGH);
  digitalWrite(RightWheel_D4, LOW);
  if(Auto_Drive)
  {
    delay(300);
    Robot_Stop();
  }
}


/*
 * Move the robot backward
 */
void Robot_Back(){
  Serial.println("Robot reversing");
  digitalWrite(LeftWheel_D1, LOW);
```

```
  digitalWrite(LeftWheel_D2, HIGH);
  digitalWrite(RightWheel_D3, LOW);
  digitalWrite(RightWheel_D4, HIGH);
}

/*
 * Function to find the distance of an ultrasonic sensor
 */
float sensor_distance() {
  float distance = 0;

  // Use the trigger pin to emit ultrasound and go into standby mode
  digitalWrite(trigPin, HIGH);
  delayMicroseconds(20);
  digitalWrite(trigPin, LOW);

  // The time the ultrasound came in, in microseconds
  // It travels 340 meters per second, which is microseconds here, and
  // This is the round trip distance, so we divide by 2.
  // It's complicated, so we can divide by 58.5.
  distance = pulseIn(echoPin, HIGH) / 58.8;
  return distance;
}

/*
 * Find the left and right distances, respectively
 */
void Detect_Object(){
  servo.write(0);
  delay(250);
  distanceRight = sensor_distance();

  servo.write(179);
  delay(250);
  distanceLeft = sensor_distance();
}

/*
 * Find the distance to the front
 */
void Detect_Front(){
  servo.write(90);
  delay(250);
  distanceFront = sensor_distance();
```

```
}
void I2C_Address_Check(){
  return;
  byte error, address;
  int nDevices;
  Serial.println("Scanning...");
  nDevices = 0;
  for(address = 1; address < 127; address++ )
  {
    Wire.beginTransmission(address);
    error = Wire.endTransmission();

    if (error == 0)
    {
      Serial.print("I2C device found at address 0x");
      if (address<16)
        Serial.print("0");
      Serial.print(address,HEX);
      Serial.println("  !");

      nDevices++;
    }
    else if (error==4)
    {
      Serial.print("Unknow error at address 0x");
      if (address<16)
        Serial.print("0");
      Serial.println(address,HEX);
    }
  }
  if (nDevices == 0)
    Serial.println("No I2C devices found\n");
  else
    Serial.println("done\n");

  delay(5000);
}

void printLCD1(String str){
    // Have them start in cell 0 of line 0.
    lcd.setCursor(0,0);
    // Print the sentence below.
    lcd.print(str);
```

```
}

void printLCD2(String str){
    // Have them start in cell 0 of line 1.
    lcd.setCursor(0,1);
    // Print the sentence below.
    lcd.print(str);
}
```